Run Girl Run!
Series III of VII
(The Bruises from My Mother's Love)

By

Author Danette

About the book

Things are beginning to get out of hand when Lunye decided to run away. She didn't think that running from her mother would take her to a place that has no rules, no love or trust. Read how Lunye finds her way to a life she wasn't prepared for.... Run Lunye! Run Girl Run!

Words to my Readers

Proverbs 6:5

Free yourself like a gazelle from the hand of the hunter, like a bird from the snare of the fowler

Acknowledgements

Even sometimes life as an adult, your suffering may not come to an end. It is my hope that this story will not only bring forth conviction, but also bring correction to many parents.

My life as an adult has had its ups and downs, but I thank God for my trials and tribulations. Because without them, I couldn't have become the person that I am today.

I trust in God that my suffering has now come to a minimum.

First off, I want to thank God.

A special thanks to my children, Tieshia, Jeffrey, Jamarr, Jessica, Terrell, Otis and Keyshawn who were there for me through good and bad times, thank you. I love you all.

I definitely want to thank my Godmother Yvette Garlington for instilling positive values in me when it counted. I will never forget her beautiful face, may she rest in peace.

I also want to thank my Godpapa William Brown a.k.a (Dub) for inspiring me with his wisdom and love. I will never forget his generosity and I will always seek to bless others as he blessed me.

Endless love to my siblings.

Last but not least, my best friend, my love, my husband, a man that has shown me what love truly feels like, Cleon Sledge... I salute him for supporting and and being my number one fan.

Hope you all enjoy...

Happy reading...!

Dedication

This is book three of the seven book series (The Bruises from My Mother's Love) is dedicated to youth and adults that can relate to the current and past pain of abuse. The burden that you carry may be heavy but know that you suffering has not gone in vain. Let your pain and your suffering become your stepping stone to your success.

Chapter 1

I know I left you guys hanging on the last book, but I had to leave you with some thoughts about the bad decision I made when I decided to get in the car with a total stranger. It taught me a valuable lesson. I do believe that God was with me the whole time throughout the whole ordeal, but it is sad that I had to be taught by experience.

I got into the car and he began to drive. Then he said, "Didn't somebody teach you never to get in the car with strangers?" That's when that weird feeling came upon me, you know, the turning of the stomach and the sick feeling, almost like a panic attack. I didn't have an answer. I was scared as hell. My lips would not move and my thought process was scrambled. As soon as the car began to move, everything inside of me wanted to open the door and make a run for it, but each time I built up the nerve, I got scared.

I watched him from my perimeter because of that weird feeling I had in my gut. There were a million thoughts running through my head in a millisecond. I began to feel my palms sweat. My anxiety amped up.

"You can let me out right here," I blurted out.

He flashed me an ugly little smile. "I can't do that."

"Why not?"

"Because I said so."

At this point, I knew I was in trouble, so I grabbed for the door, but I had a hard time finding the handle. That gave him time to lock the doors from the driver's side. Now I know at this point that my life was over. He had turned his back to the driver's seat window and was staring at me, beads of sweat formulating on his forehead. He kept biting his bottom lip soft enough to not break the skin. The thoughts in my head were racing so fast I felt faint.

It was time for defense mode. I had my legs ready to kick and my hands were ready to gouge his damn eyes out. He finally stopped staring and said, "I want you to suck my dick."

Every muscle in my body tensed up. My words would not form after hearing him say "suck his dick."

"Bitch, didn't you hear me?"

I was still in shock and could not respond. My brain kept signaling my hands and legs to attack, but they were both unresponsive. I finally blurted out, "I want to go home!"

"It's too late for that now," he said. "You should have thought about that before you got your hot ass in my car."

"I am only thirteen years old!"

"Yeah, sure you are!" He laughed and told me to take off my pants. Then I began screaming that I had gonorrhea. I thought maybe that might change his mind about raping me.

"I don't give a fuck, bitch. Pull your panties down now, before I kill you and leave your ass in this alley."

Chapter 1

I began to cry; I called on God to help me. That's when he pulled out a small knife and grabbed the back of my hair and put the knife up to my neck. I just knew I was about to die. I was so scared that he cut me and I didn't even notice. I thought I was sweating when I felt the drops falling from my neck. I didn't notice it was blood until I saw the blood on his hand. I then felt my life slipping away. I called on my unseen friend. You know, the one that I could see, but no one else could. Well anyway, I was dying at this point and the first person I could think of was my unseen friend. I closed my eyes and grabbed hold to every muscle in my body. I screamed out, "Please help me, I am about to die.' I opened my eyes and the man looked as if he'd seen a ghost... All of a sudden, he removed his hand from my hair and pulled back the knife.

"Get the fuck out of my car!"

I was puzzled for a moment, you would think that I would have torn ass out of that car, but I was scared to move. I stared at him for a minute or so until he said "Look, I am not going to tell you again, get the fuck out of my car!"

I heard the locks pop on the car doors and I slowly grabbed for the handle. I never took my eyes off of him because I thought it was a trick. It felt like it took me a long time to open the door, but I finally heard that sound of freedom. The door flew open and I slowly slid backwards. He looked as if he was getting irritated. I saw his hands coming towards me and all I could think was that I knew it was a trick. I just knew he was about to grab me and rape me, but he didn't; he pushed me out the car and I hit the ground. I was so scared I didn't even feel any pain. He then yelled out to me, "Close my damn door and take you young ass home before somebody find you stankin!"

I got up and closed his door. He called me a dumb young bitch and sped off down the alley. I sat there for a few minutes, still in shock. I came back to reality when I realized I heard some damn rats. I got up and ran so damn fast I couldn't see my surroundings. I ran until my legs contacted my brain and signaled them to stop. I was out of breath and my heart was beating so fast and loud I couldn't hear nothing.

Chapter 2

After I caught my breath and my heart returned to a normal rhythm, I found myself crying. I cried so hard, my tears were burning my face and didn't stop until I had no tears left, I then realized I could have been dead. I began to feel a wet substance coming down my neck. I guess I was so happy to be free I forgot that pervert cut my neck. I imagined it was a big cut, I thought I needed stitches but there was no way I was going to the hospital and risk getting caught and be sent back to my mother's house. I truly had nowhere to go and no one to turn to.

I decided to examine the cut on my neck. I thought would be a life threatening, but when I touched it very gently, it wasn't life threatening at all. The cut was very small and it was bleeding as if I had been sliced with a sword. Well maybe I was over exaggerating because I was scared. Now I knew I wasn't going to die my mind was at ease. I grabbed the bottom of my shirt and dabbed it on my neck to wipe away the blood. I knew at some point that I would have to get some type of water or peroxide to clean it. Alcohol was not an option because that shit burns. I finally got my thoughts together. Now it was time to get to a safe place and get myself cleaned up.

As I walked, I found myself in tears once again asking myself, "Why is my life so hard?" I didn't have an answer but the thought lingered in my head like a clothing hanger. Before I knew it, I found myself back in the neighborhood where I lived with my mother. Panic invaded my body and I wanted to turn around, but somehow, I didn't.

I remembered a place that was somewhat secluded and safe. I walked toward this building a friend of mine told me that they used to hang out and drink and kick it. I remembered being there once before. We all hung out on the back porch and they would drink eight ball, you know, that was the popular beer back then and a lot of teens were drinking it. I'd tried it before and it was disgusting to me. I never understood why they enjoyed it so much. Buy hey, who was I to judge? I finally got to the back of the building and somehow felt a sense of peace. I began to walk up the back porch stairs, trying to make my way to the third floor. After the first couple of stairs, my body tensed up and began to hurt. I couldn't understand how this came about, but I fought through the pain and finally made it to the third floor. I was so tired that I melted on the stairs, I don't even remember sitting down.

I looked up at the sky and saw how beautiful and peaceful it looked. I was thinking to myself how can a world be so beautiful but so hurtful? I sporadically thought about my mother. This time I envisioned her from a different perspective. I imagined her in tears, mumbling how she missed me. When she comes home I am going to tell her how much I love her and how much I missed her. I remember smiling, and then reality kicked in, my fictional thoughts disappeared. I was awaked by a memory of her calling me a black bitch, saying I would never be nothing. I guess the mind can only take you so far into a fairytale until the truth reminds you of reality.

Before I knew it, the sounds of the birds chirping and the sun beaming on my face awakened me. I didn't even remember going

Chapter 2

to sleep. I must have been extremely tired for me to do something like that, especially after what happened to me. It was time to move on from the honeycomb hideout because I didn't want no one to come out of their place and catch me just chilling on the back porch like a homeless bum—even though I was homeless. I was on my journey again, with nowhere to go, I was tired, hungry and I felt filthy. I was getting desperate.

The thought of going home crossed my mind a couple of times, but I was scared. I walked until I was tired and I met up with some Hispanic people that I didn't know too well but well enough to stop and start a conversation. I just needed to rest my feet and I knew if I sat with a group I wouldn't be noticed. I walked up and blurted out *'Que pasa?'* They seemed pretty cool, well let's just say for the moment. They asked me if I wanted to make some money and I was like, hell yeah! I didn't think about it at the time. Maybe I should've asked, what they wanted me to do. But I guess I was just too thirsty to realize it was a trick. I made a bad mistake because I was in a bad situation.

I followed them when it was time to go on this mission even though I never even knew what it was, but by their conversation, I knew it was illegal. So, that cat was out the bag. I was supposed to be an accessory to a burglary. Now, I knew what I was participating in, I just didn't care at the time because I also just knew I wasn't going to get caught. It crossed my mind for a moment that it could all possibly go wrong, but my thoughts were interrupted by two of the guys arguing.

As I grasped hold of the moment, I realized those fools were trying to fight right before a burglary. I am not experienced in crime but I have common sense and my common sense tells me that we need to be alert and focused. I was on the verge of saying something, but common sense kicked again. I just needed to shut the hell up. It wouldn't have taken much for one of their tough asses to knock the hell out of me and I was pretty sure that one them fools would have tried to show out, so I just did what any person with common sense would have done—shut up. Well, we must have been getting close because everybody started to quiet down. From that point on, I felt my palms sweat with every step.

Finally, one of the guys stopped and turned to us and said, "This is what we are going do. We are going to open the side window and we gonna slide her through the window so she can open the door,"

I looked around. Of course I was the only female and that meant he was talking about me. I starting to get the bubble guts and I was just plain ole scared. I knew there was no turning back, I had to follow through because I didn't want to be labeled lame and besides, they would have beat my ass. The ass kicking was the deal breaker, so I followed through with their plan. One of the guys lifted the window to the basement and I knew it was show time. I felt as if I was moving in slow motion because of my hesitance about to commit a crime. I squatted down and slid my right leg in the window. I felt my bones popping as I slid my left leg right behind my right leg. As I began to slide the rest of my body through, I could feel the window pane scraping my belly and my chest. I remember scraping the bottom of my chin as I slid the rest of me inside. Both of my feet hit the floor. I looked around; all I could smell was fabric softener. It smelled so fresh and the house was clean. My thoughts were interrupted by one of the guys. "Hurry up and come open the door." I had to get back on track. The door was just a few steps away. I had to unlock it; it was almost as if it was jammed. I kept hearing them say, "What the hell? Are you fuckin stupid? Open the fucking door!" Being in a strange place, committing a crime and someone constantly

Chapter 2

calling you names while rushing you to open a damn door made me even more uncomfortable.

It seemed like about thirty minutes went past, but it was only like, five minutes. All of a sudden, it got quiet. I heard some running and I damn near melted. I didn't know what to do; I knew that they were running because someone was coming. I tried opening the door again but I heard someone coming and I ran towards the window that I came in. I tried to jump up and get through the window but I must have slipped because I ended up on the floor. Before I knew it, I felt the presence of someone I didn't want to be there, I heard the sound of a Hispanic man's voice.

"What the fuck are you doing in my crib?"

I had no answer for him at all. I just wanted to get out of that window as quickly as possible, but given the circumstances, I wasn't going to make it. I tried to get up. My brain signaled the rest of my body to make a run for it, but shit didn't go as planned because that Hispanic man grabbed me from the back of my shirt and slammed me to the floor. Then he had the nerve to sit on me while some lady called the police. I tried to talk my way out of the situation, but that man was not hearing it. While we were waiting on the police, he kept asking me who those guys were, because I was going to go to jail by myself. I really didn't care; I'd learned the no-snitch rule from the streets early in the game and I did not want to deal with the consequences. The Hispanic man didn't let up. Before I knew it, I heard some walkie talkies and I knew that was the police. I was terrified because that meant they had to contact my mother and that meant an ass whipping I would never forget. My bowels awoke abruptly. I had to shit, to be more precise. I heard the footsteps get closer and my escape was out of the question unless Superman showed up. The knock at the door caused a gas intrusion, and I farted. I don't think no one even heard anything. The lady that called the cops was there to open the door and the whole environment changed once I heard the sound. The walkie talkies were getting closer and the sound of my heartbeat became louder. The sound of their shoes was so loud that I was able to count the steps as they got closer. Silence filled the room momentarily once the officers entered. I was praying it was all a nightmare but I knew that it was no point of pinching myself because I knew damn well I was awake

The police broke the silence by saying "Do you know that you are going to jail?"

"I didn't do nothing."

The officer said, "I'm sure you're innocent and so are the other one hundred thousand criminals."

I then decided to just shut the hell up and deal with the consequences because there was no talking my way out of it. The walk to the police car seemed to last forever. For every step I took, it felt like I took three steps back. So, there I was, a criminal on my way to the big house. Well, of course I am exaggerating, but I felt that way in that moment. I was scared and nervous at the same time because when I was put in the back of that car, I felt like I was getting in a car trunk or something. The seats were cold and I was very sensitive to the touch. The sound of the car door slamming caused my stomach muscles to tighten and my bowels began to growl. All of the sudden I had to take a shit again. Now I really have a problem because I'm handcuffed from behind and sitting in the back of a police car and my bowels were ready to put in some work. Yeah, I know that's disgusting, but look here, I am just telling it like it is and trying to be as detailed as possible. The police car smelled almost like a musty basement. My thoughts were moving so fast I didn't even pay attention when the police started the car and pulled off. I only took notice when we hit a

Chapter 2

bump, because I was ready to release my bowels. The handcuffs were making it difficult to concentrate on holding my bowels, so I did what I had to do. I dislocated my thumbs and removed the handcuffs. Now I felt like I had regained my control back now it was time to meditate and focus on holding bowels because I would be very embarrassed if I shit in my pants. Back to reality, I am going to jail and all I could think about was the sight of my mother's face. I was more scared of her than jail. In my mind I was thinking, "just take me to jail and leave me there. I would be better off." Time flew by pretty fast because we were pulling up to the police station. I became very nervous.

"Are y'all calling my mother ?"

The police officer replied, "Yes. You are a minor and if you tell us who was with you, we will let you go home with your mother."

I said in my head. "I guess I won't be going home tonight."

Chapter 3

There I was, in the garage of the police station; that's all I could see were police cars, police wagons and detective cars. My heart was pounding so fast it started to sound like a juke mix or something. The car stopped and even though the police were talking, I managed to tune them out, because I was just that scared. My thoughts were interrupted by the front doors slamming and followed by the sound of one of them opening my door. The officer was sure I knew the procedure, but everything got out of hand when they noticed that I no longer had on the handcuffs. All I remember is the officers became very aggressive and one of them slammed me into the car while the other one grabbed my arms and began to put the handcuffs back on me but he went a little too far. He punched me multiple times as if I were resisting arrest. Okay, after being punched and the handcuffs so tight, you think I would shut the hell up, but that wasn't an option. I just had to voice my opinion about their aggressive behavior. I said to them: "Why would you punch me?"

One of the officers said, "Because I can."

I wasn't prepared for that, so I just started to cry. At that time, it was the best rebuttal. I had no other defense that would put me in control. I was on my way to the big house and no one to call on

Chapter 3

or no one that really cared, anyway. My only worry was having to go back home to my mother.

Inside, the smell of the police station was almost toxic, like a mixture of butt sweat, cigarettes and typewriter ink. I know you may find it difficult to imagine that as a smell, but combined together trust me, it's not pleasant. After leading me to the room where I guess they were going to process me, I began to panic; my heart was beating slow/fast. That's when you become so scared you don't know if your heart is beating slow or fast. Sometimes that feeling causes serious issues to my colon.

Speaking of colon, I had to drop the kids off at the pool. I know you are thinking what the hell? Well, just say I was trying to be cute about taking a dump. Not to get off track I was nervous as hell. I had so many thoughts racing through my head and they were all bumping into each other. One the officers came in and said. "Her mother said she is a runaway and a habitual liar. She said send her to jail because she wasn't coming to get her."

They didn't know that was like music to my ears. I was going to jail. I didn't have to worry about getting the crap beat out of me. Jail would be my new home. I didn't even think I was about to be locked up with some real criminals. Besides, it didn't matter; it's not like I had a choice. I sat down, and asked, "When when are y'all taking me to jail? I'm hungry and tired." Furthermore, I was tired of smelling their funky asses anyway. One of the officers looked back at me.

"Shut the hell up. You will get there soon enough." Everything in my body wanted to say something smart, but common sense kicked in and put me in my place.

Finally, I was instructed to get up and they removed the one of the handcuffs from the wall and connected it to my other hand.

I didn't know where I was going. All I knew was I was ready to go. I rode in a police paddy wagon. It wasn't the most attractive thing to ride in or the safest. I should have been in a seatbelt or something because my body was thrown from left to right, it was quite difficult to hold my balance in handcuffs.

Well, I guessed I was at my new home because the paddy wagon stopped for quite some time. I heard the officers get out of the paddy wagon. The sound of their voices for some reason became annoying to me. I closed my eyes tight and tried to block the sound but I was distracted by the sound of that loud ass door opening. I looked at the officers as if I was going to kick their asses but I got my shit together I was trying to make my out of the wagon but it was kind of difficult because I wasn't able to use my hands. Trust me, the officers didn't offer help nor did they give a damn. I finally made it out and the first thing I did was use my nose to smell the area to get a better idea of my surroundings. It almost smelled like a musty basement mixed with the smell of a printer. That smell will never leave my memory. I was handled a lil' rough for someone that was not giving them any problems. However, my skin was tough, thanks to good old mom. I could take an ass whipping with no problem. I am not saying it was a good thing, but it enhanced my tolerance level.

So, now I was being escorted through the 1100 S. Hamilton and I was in big trouble. As we were walking through the station, one of the officers had his hand on the cuffs behind my back, guiding me or maybe he was restraining me because in case I felt the urge to run. And to be completely honest, I did think of running but my brain and my thoughts were not getting along because my brain was surely using protective logic: If I ran, there was a possibility of me getting shot or something. I felt I was being pushed, but hey, it's not like anyone cared or was going to rescue me. That much I was

Chapter 3

used to. We finally made it to the office where they were taking me. At this point, my heart was beating faster than a second hand on a clock. Speaking of clocks, I was told to stand under the clock until they were ready for me. I didn't quite understand why I had to stand under a clock but they must have told many people the same thing because there was a worn piece of tape that formed a line right below the clock. It seemed as if I stood there for hours. All I could hear was the sound of a typewriter and a few irrelevant conversations. Finally, one of the officers came over to me and told me to turn around and face the wall. Well, it wasn't like it was a choice, so I turned around and kept my mind focused on freedom. I know it almost seemed strange that I would focus on freedom when I was going to jail, but I did what I had to do at the time. It was about time for me to be processed in. I was informed to remove all my clothes. That made me suspicious because I'd never experienced this before unless I was being abused. I tried to cover my body as I stood there with my underwear on. I felt disgusting but I thank God that those other officers were gone. The new folks that took over looked a tad bit militant. I am not sure if they were officers or what, I just knew they were in charge and that was more than enough info for me.

One of the ladies walked over to me and said, "Put your damn hands down, we all got the same thing up in here." She made me feel weird; I am not sure exactly how, but I felt strange for a moment. I felt like I didn't have control. I hated her in that instant and didn't understand why. That nervous feeling dominated my whole body and my mind was on auto pilot. I heard her talking, but my mind was in charge of all my responses. I slowly removed my hands from my body and put them on my sides as if I was in the military until she told me to take off my underwear. I panicked and tears rolled down my face. I began to shake and I remember the lady looking at me as if she'd seen a ghost. I didn't want to take off my underwear because I was didn't know what was going to happen next.

"We are not here to hurt you, "she said in a soft, yet stern voice. "I need you to remove your underwear for your safety and ours."

It's almost like someone took over her body momentarily; it was strange but I felt a sense of peace and I removed my underwear. I did not feel comfortable, but I didn't feel like I was in danger. I was at the beginning stage of getting hair on my petunia(vagina) down there. I wanted to cover that part but I had to have my hands to the sides. Standing there with my private area exposed made me feel anxious and violated. Even though the process wasn't that long, it felt like a lifetime. The other girls seemed to be a little more comfortable than me. Maybe there were a few that were timid. I was beyond timid, I was scared as hell. We all were given these outfits that almost looked like doctor scrubs but without the V-neck. They were blue and we were given some big granny panties and they were white. I don't remember them having tags on them they could've been used but they were white in the crotch so I had no complaints. We were instructed to walk towards the shower area and take a shower and put on the jail suits. At this point I didn't care; I just want to put some damn clothing on because I felt like somebody was looking at me. Besides, I may have been extremely paranoid, but I wasn't able to determine what was going on because I was so distracted by being naked. Finally, it was my turn to shower. The vision that I had was totally different from what I encountered. I walked into the shower and nothing was adding up. My nerves began to wake up and perform; the brick walls from the shower began to start closing and my heart began to beat really fast, so fast that it became the only rhythm I was able to hear. I walked toward the showers and it was like a brick wall with many shower heads on it and there were no shower curtains for privacy. I removed my

Chapter 3

shower shoes and walked under the water slowly because I had to make sure the temperature was to my liking because me and cold water just don't click at bathing time. The floors were cold and they almost felt like walking on concrete. They gave us a small piece of soap, almost like those small pieces of soap the hotels give you. I had no room to be picky because I hadn't washed my tail in two days, so this was a blessing. I finally adapted to the water and I began washing my body but for some reason I keep washing my petunia and my tiny boobies. I believe I was trying to hide myself from the other girls. This girl next to me that I saw from my side eye view had bigger boobies than me and she had a big ole jello booty. I found it kind of creepy that I didn't want anyone to look at me but here I was, comparing our body parts. My thoughts were interrupted by the sound of a forced fart, the reason I say forced fart is it sounded forced. I know you may be thinking, how do you determine if someone forced out a fart? Trust me; it's from many years of experience. Which brought me back to the time when me and my brother used to play fart games, one of us would fart and the other would say chex and cross our finger but if you got caught slipping and didn't say chex, yo ass had the fart touch. At the time, it was fun for me and my lil brother because we didn't have much fun to look forward to. As I abandoned that memory I came to reality and protected my sense of smell because I know when there is a fart there is a smell. I didn't just cover my nose I cut off all inhaling through my nose and utilized my mouth to take small breaths. I know this sounds weird, but at the time I thought I was protecting myself. I heard a loud voice that scared me so bad I farted my own damn self.

"Let's go ladies." I was glad it wasn't as loud as the other girl's because when she did it, she had an audience and they responded. I looked around the shower to make sure no one noticed anything. As I walked out my mind automatically told my hands to cover my petunia, forgetting my hands were supposed to be held on my sides. As I walked past, one the staff yelled at me really loud,

"Put your hands at your sides!" I got so nervous I dropped everything. For a moment, I thought how the hell I was going to pick this stuff up? The other girls were looking at me like I was about to perform. If you really think about it, squatting down to pick up things will expose some things. "Pick your things up and let's get moving!"

I bent over to pick up the soap and towel so fast I don't think you would have caught if it were in slow motion. We all went the area where we put on our jail cell outfits. I was so damn happy, I believe I was dressed before everyone. I felt so much better and my private areas are back secure. Were we then given a blanket, a shee , roll on deodorant, a tooth brush, a few bars of soap and a small thing of toothpaste. I was not impressed at all with the little hygiene bag they gave us. We were then escorted to where we would be residing. We had to walk and not talk, listen and do what we were told to do or suffer the consequences. No one truly knew the consequences, but I knew I didn't want to find out.

We all did what we were told, except these two nappy-headed lil girls who were talking and laughing like this was the norm for them, We made it to the elevators, but this didn't look like a normal elevator, it was huge and silver and scary. We were all told get on the elevator and face the back and put our hands on the back and lock them together. A strange and unfamiliar stench filled the air and it instantly gave me a headache. It was a short ride and that was a relief, because I felt like I was about to pass out. The elevator doors opened. I was short of breath and began to panic. Then I heard the staff yell, "Turn around, step out from the wall and face it. And I don't expect to hear any noise."

Chapter 3

I just forgot everything that I was feeling before that moment. I just wanted to get where I was going so that I could get me some rest and cry in peace. We stood facing that wall for a long time. I began to count the bricks and for a moment, I forgot where I was, but I was reminded when I heard, "Turn to your right and walk slowly with your hands locked behind you."

As we walked down that long hall I had time to explore. The cell block was huge and somewhat musty, but clean, I caught a glimpse of my reflection on the glass windows we were walking past. Wow! I was an official convict. I felt confused, wondering, how did I get here and why. I had no answers. I wondered what the other girls were thinking. Did they have the same thoughts as me, or was I the only person to care that I was a jail bird?

"STOP!" We all stopped so suddenly we bumped into each other. We were led in by the staff and again, we had to line up under the clock. I thought to myself, like, what's up with lining up under clocks all the time? Of course, we did what we were told because we had no choice. We waited and waited until we were assigned to our cells. I walked over to my cell and I was quite disappointed in what I saw. I couldn't believe what I walked into. The room was the size of a closet, with a box and a thin mattress on top of it. There were freakin bricks everywhere. I couldn't focus when I I walked in the room and saw the sink on top of the damn toilet. You would think I would be more appreciative, considering my circumstances. I put my bedding on the bed and sat down. I noticed they had a small desk in the room with a chair. I couldn't think of a reason for a desk and chair to be in a cell. I thought, maybe it's for us to write letters I didn't really care at the time, I just laid down and stared at the ceiling, trying to figure out my next move. I focused my thoughts on the toilet again. Why would they put those two together? Why would they want us to drink toilet water? Is the water really coming from the toilet? I was thirsty, but I was not going to drink from that toilet/sink. All of a sudden, I heard a loud noiseit was the sound of the doors locking. For some reason I was okay with this because I had no worries of anyone trying to hurt me. As the night went on, I lost track of time and I fell asleep for a short time and when I woke up, I almost forgot I was in jail. It was so dark and I felt myself becoming anxious. I began to cry silently because I did not want anyone to hear me; they probably would have thought I was a lame. Even though I cried silently, my cry was loud enough to shake the city.

Chapter 4

The sound of the cells waking, along with some women yelling, "it's time to clean your cells, ladies". I sat up on the bed with the ugliest frown on my face, disappointed because I was hoping all this was a dream. I got up and fixed my sheet and my blanket on my bed. This was something I was really good at because my mom taught me well. If my bed wasn't made right she would snatch the covers back and make me do it again. After I was done making the bed, I glanced over at my toothbrush and toothpaste having thoughts of brushing my teeth, but the water looked as if it was coming from the toilet and that just didn't sit well with me. I thought that I could put that on hold, until I could find some regular sink water. There was not much for me to do in my room, so I walked over to the door and pushed it open. I saw the girls standing on the side of their cells, so I assumed I was supposed to do the same thing. I was right because eventually we all were standing next to our cells. The cell doors locked and we were all instructed to stand along the wall so we could have breakfast. I looked around the entire room and my anxiety began to take control, my palms began to sweat and my stomach began to turn upside down. The walls were closing in and the bricks seemed like they got so much closer, I felt like I could almost touch them. Before I could think any further, I heard a loud voice."Ladies, line up. It's time to eat. At least this distracted me for a while; it took my mind off what was going on around me because that's one of my favorite times of the day to eat. Yes, I know I am greedy but I would say I just enjoy food.

Well, the food wasn't to much to brag on. We had a boiled egg, toast, some corn flakes, and milk. My attention was brought to the milk only because the milk was stored in this big silver thing and it had a nozzle on it almost like a water machine and it had a silver pitcher to match. As I was getting my food, one of the girls said, 'This all we get?' and of course I ignored her because I didn't know her. But that didn't stop her from talking; she kept ranting about her going home and getting up out of there. I heard her talking, I tuned out, because she was talking too much. I was really trying to focus on watching everybody else. Some of those girls looked like grown ups. I walked over to the eating area and sat down and looked at my food and I was grateful because I remembered days when I didn't have nothing to eat. I spread butter on my toast and slapped the tiny container of jelly on it too, I cracked my boiled egg and peeled the shell. I was used to rinsing them off once I peeled them but I was too damn scared to even ask to rinse them off and furthermore, no one else seemed to want to ask either.

The days after that passed in slow motion. I just learned to adapt because I didn't have much to look forward to. I was there only about a week or so. Even though I loved my little brother and sisters, they belonged to my mother and I could not compete with her. So I tried to forget anything that was associated with family because I knew my mother controlled that territory.

I was reminded of my court day by one of the staff. I wasn't happy by a long shot because ther was a possibility of me going home. The thought of me going home made me panic and lose my appetite, and that day in particular seemed to move so fast I

Chapter 4

thought I was living my life in fast motion because all I remember is playing cards with a few of the girls and we went to church and we got these huge Snickers bars. I was so stressed out I couldn't even eat it. I believe I was the only one who didn't eat mine. This girl named Lisa was a straight bully. She was in for stealing and she was big and ugly; you could look at her and could tell she could do you some damage. I never really crossed paths with her until that day after we came from church. Everybody was talking stuff because I didn't eat my candy yet and they were cracking jokes. Normally I would joke around and laugh with them but this day was not the day I wanted to be bothered. I made it perfectly clear that I wasn't in the mood for fun and games and then Lisa walked toward me.

"Gimme that candy bar." I looked at her as if I wasn't in the mood. Calm as hell, she said, "I'm not playing, give it to me."

Now my brain it recognizing could see on her face that she was in bully mode.

"I'm eating my shit later." I said the curse word because I felt that it would intimidate her somewhat. Well it didn't work. Instead it made her mad.

"I will beat your ass and take your shit." I sat there in silence for at least thirty seconds. I was stuck because this girl was huge and I was not ready for what was to come. "You ate yours and I want to eat mine, too." All I knew was she was ready to rob me of my only satisfaction of the day and I was not going at gun point. I mentally prepared myself for battle. In my mind, I was gonna win this fight because I was not going to give up my candy bar.

She started to come closer and I knew this was going to get physical. So, I quickly scanned the room for help. Just in time,

Ms Martin was close to my aid, so I yelled out, "Ms Martin, what time is group?" I had to act fast. I was no match for Lisa. Ms Martin replied, "Let's see." She grabbed a book from the staff desk and walked over, just like I wanted her to. This disappointed Lisa because her plan to eat my Snickers was put to an immediate stop when Ms Martin came over. *Yes!* I took that opportunity at that moment to eat my candy bar. It wasn't as good as it could have been because I didn't eat it when I wanted to. But at least Lisa didn't get it and eat it her damn self. I was not sure if she was over it a but at that point I really didn't give a damn because the next time I was going to fight her ass.

It was time for school. I didn have a clue that we would be going to school in jail. School was different in jail; it's definitely not what I expected. I wasn't used to seeing everyone with the same thing on and the desk and the chairs had gang signs written all over them. The cool thing was, we were able to see the guys. Yep, school was co-ed and those girls would come with their lips shining and their jail uniforms almost looked as if they were starched or something. I didn't see too much pleasure in trying to be cute because we were all in jail. Until one day in particular. As I walked down the hall once we got off the elevator, I felt different—almost as if I was going to have a great day.

Once we made it to our class we lined up outside of the room until we were told to go into class and there he was, Renzo, yes, my first love, I saw him before he saw me. I was nervous because I was looking like I just didn't care about myself. I sat down in the first seat I saw and immediately the teacher told me to get up and walk to the end of the row., Now this brought attention to me. I tried to play it off and look straight ahead as if I didn't see him. When he loked my way, it almost felt like he had lasers in his eyes.

Chapter 4

I could have sworn I felt heat on my body. I eyeballed him down from my side view because I didn't want to miss nothing. The first thing I saw when he turned his head were those beautiful brown eyes and that nappy ponytail. I didn't care because he was just fine to me.

I heard a noise, almost like *spnppppssssh!* I knew deep down in my soul that was him trying to get my attention. I continued to play it off and act like I didn't hear a thing and took my seat. I looked straight forward the whole time in class with the most simple smile on my face. Time flew past so fast, all I knew is I was day dreaming one moment and then it was time to go. I regretted every moment after I saw him because I knew that I really wanted to hug him and tell him how much I missed him. We weren't able to do those things , but I would have done it anyway because I didn't know how to handle that weird, mushy feeling anyway. As me and the girls lined up on the brick wall, one of them passed me a note and said "Renzo said give this to you.' I was so damn happy I almost forgot we were in jail and was about to open the note. This girl name Rachel, she was an Audi home veteran, whispered for me to put it in my panties, so I did what came naturally and listened to her advice. I put that note in my panties so fast, I didn't even see myself do it.

I swear, the journey back to our tier was the longest. I kept imagining what he had written, but my thoughts were interrupted by the sound of the staff telling us to go in and stand by the wall and extend our arms to the side. This was done each and every time we left the tier. Believe it or not, those girls will find a way to sneak some shit in, because a woman's body have plenty of pockets, if you know what I mean.

When the staff came over to me, I was so nervous I could feel the sweat form under my armpits. My heart was moving so fast it almost sounded like it was outside of my chest. As she patted me down, everything in the inside of me wanted to melt but of course that was not an option, so I just stood there hoping she wouldn't find the note. What took every bit of one minute felt like an hour. Finally, she took her business over to the next girl and the girl before looked at me and I looked her with a sigh of relief. The search was finally over and we were instructed to go to our cells. It was quiet time, which really meant they were about to change shifts. Well, this worked out for me because this gave me an opportunity to read my note from Renzo.

I made it to my cell and the anticipation drove me crazy because I had to sit on the bed until they did room check. My cell was the one all the way on the end. Everything inside of me just wanted to pull out that note and read it really fast, but I just couldn't take a chance on getting caught. The staff came in my room and she looked at me kinda weird. I didn't have a clue why she made me feel weird, I just wanted her out so I could finally read my note. She walked toward the door and I was so happy until she turned back around.

"Whatever you are up to, you will get caught so do don't anthing stupid." I really didn't care about anything this lady was saying because my focus was soley on the note. I just looked at her puzzled, as if she was crazy or something and she just walked out of the cell. I thought about what she said and I looked at it as a warning, so I laid down and waited to read the note because I didn't want to get caught. I waited and I waited; I thought maybe they were watching me. I heard a lot of talking outside my cell and I knew this was the time to read my note because the shift was changing. I dug it out and the first thing I did was smell it to see if I could smell his scent on it. But all I could smell is pencil and my own scent. I opened it as if it was a certified letter from the

Chapter 4

president. Finally, I saw his handwriting and it was so beautiful to me.I It read:

Dear Lunye, I don't know why you didn't want to talk to me today, you acted like you didn't see me. I miss you and it is so messed up the way you left me. I want to hug you and kiss you. I thought your momma hurt you or something. When we get out of this place I want you to come live with me and my mom and you will be safe.

And the note ended with I love you, see you tomorrow at school. I smiled and held the note up to my chest, A tear rolled down my cheek. Before I knew it, tears were everywhere. I couldn't stop crying and I just wanted to feel him hug me because he was my superman. All I could do is think about him and cry, because he was all I had. I needed to be consoled so I had to tune in to my unseen friend; I hadn't spoke to him in awhile. I guess maybe because I was so distracted with all this jail shit.

It's very weird how I communicated with my unseen friend. He don't have a name, he just appears when things go really bad and I need him. I cried out to him because I had some emotions that I couldn't explain. He appeared and I was worried for a minute because I had not communicated with him for awhile. I began to cry and share my thoughts with my friend. I didn't understand why I couldn't be normal. I wanted to be home and be able to see Renzo, I wanted to go to a normal school and be happy with my friends. For some reason, after all that venting my friend did not respond, so I began to cry even harder. I got up and walked over to the desk in my cell and I sat in the chair and just stared at the desk and I glanced over to the paper and pencil everything in me wanted to grab that pencil and paper and just write, but I was then distracted by the carvings on the desk. Someone carved 'I hate myself 'multiple times. There were many different gang signs on there, too, but my focus was on the one that said I hate myself like, ten times. I was drawn to it because I was really feeling that way at that moment. I wondered who that person was, and why they felt that way. The sound of the locks unlocking on the door scared the hell out of me and I knew it was time to come out. As I walked out the door, I noticed someone new was on the tier. It was a really young girl she looked about nine or ten years old and she was Caucasion. I was thinking, what the heck is she doing in here? One of the girls asked her what her name was.

"Amber."

"How old are you?"

"Ten."

"Why you in here, Amber?"

I wasn't ready for what this little girl had to say. Amber was proud to announce she was in for stabbing her mother eleven times.

I stared at her. "You killed your mother?"

"Nope, the bitch didn't die."

I felt a need to sit alone because that was too much for my brain. I found myself sitting on the day couch by the television. I began to daydream and imagine myself killing my mother and it just didn't give me any satisfaction at all. I just couldn't imagine myself hurting her. But then I wondered, how can I not want to hurt her, but she seems to always want to hurt me?

I remembered she was on top of me one day, she was hitting me the spit from her mouth showering my face. I could feel the pressure from her body on my chest, feeling like I was about to break in half. All I could hear at the time was bitch, bitch, bitch.

Chapter 4

I mean those weren't the only words she was saying, it was just that word was like a stain on my brain. I just felt like I was cursed, like I was a mistake or something.

I heard it the locks click. That meant it was close to our bedtime. I was ready to go to bed anyway because I was going to court tomorrow and for some odd reason, I felt the need to go home. I never really felt this way and it was kinda weird to me but hey crazier things have happened. I walked over to my cell and stood next to it and slid down the brick wall until my butt hit the floor. I knew damn well if I just decided to open the cell door and walk in, I would have gotten in big trouble. I sat there about five minutes or so until I heard the staff say, "Bedtime! Ladies, let's move!" I was so damn happy, I got up the same way I sat down, but in reverse, I slid up the brick wall and made my way to my cell. I immediately flopped on my bed and began to think about the possibility of going home. After hearing what Amber did to her mom I just couldn't imagine myself getting to that point.

My thoughts shifted quickly. I began to think about Renzo again because he made me feel warm inside and he made me smile. I heard a loud noise like a hammer hitting some pipes in the wall and I heard some people talking like they were yelling or something. Then I realized that it was the way girls and guys communicated in there. I thought this was cool and I tried to yell out, but no one payed me any attention, so I did the next best thing and shut up and did my own thing. I grab the note that Renzo gave me. I was thinking how stupid I was for pretending not to see him. Yes, I was rather childish but at the time I didn't care, I thought I was cool. But I must say I was regretting it. Before I knew it, I was sound asleep.

Chapter 5

I was awakened by the smell of coffee coming from the staff room. I wasn't able to determine what time it was, because I didn't have a clock and looking up at the window didn't help because it was still kinda dark, but the smell of the coffee told me it was the morning. I walked over to the door and stood there, just watching. The door had a really thick glass door surrounded by metal. I'm assuming that's all glass so the staff can keep an eye on us. I had an anxious feeling. I was ready to go, but on the other hand, I knew I would not be able to see Renzo. But it was out of my control. I finally walked over to my desk and decided to take a seat. I grabbed the pencil and the paper, and started to write a letter to Renzo with plans of giving the letter to one of the girls and hoping they could get it to him.

I started it over multiple times because I couldn't give a letter that was sloppy. I decided not to write at all because I was nervous and I really couldn't think. The only words that came to my mind were I love you. I couldn't explain why; I truly didn't even know what love was at the time. All I knew is that he made me feel special. I began to write his name and then drew a heart around it. I wrote my name all over that sheet of paper. I then began to sporadically just write my thoughts down, and before you know it, I filled up all five sheets of paper front and back. I didn't even feel overwhelmed. I actually felt a moment

Chapter 5

of peace as I shared my thoughts on those five sheets of paper. I heard the locks unlock and I only saw a few girls come out and we came earlier than normal and I am sure our doors unlocked early because we all had court that day. I walked over to the clock, because I knew without doing this I wouldn't be eating at all. Of course I was the first person in line because I was hungry and my stomach was hurting because I was really nervous about court. Breakfast was terrible as usual; one boiledegg, a piece of toast and a glass of milk. I ate my breakfast and and it was time to get prepared for court. The clock showed seven-thirty and court was at nine am. I just knew I had to look nice so I would not be looked at as an animal. I even put on some good ole lip shine; it was actually the vaseline the staff gave me for my hair. I was ready to rock and roll. Time was definitely on my side because a few minutes after getting my self together I heard the staff calling us to line up. I moved rapidly because I just wanted to go because this place just wasn't for me. I didn't feel like I fit in. No matter how comfortable I tried to get, I had it in my mind that I was going to go home and be the perfect kid. I was going to clean and be at her begging call. Boy! I had big plans. I wanted to give my mom plenty of hugs, but there was a tiny voice inside of me saying it won't work; you know your mom does not like you. I ignored it because I really loved her, I just didn't like her. I got some advice from some of the girls in jail, they showed me how to make my clothing look good and have no wrinkles without using an iron. We weren't allowed irons and things like that because they could be used as weapons. The girls showed me how to fold my jail uniform and lay it under my mattress and when I put it on, it looked like I actually ironed it. I was looking good and very neat. I knew this would attract my mom's attention if had myself together. She loved for everthing to be really neat and clean. It was kind of weird because she wanted us to clean daily. She would have us to clean things that were already clean. At this point I didn't care about her flaws, I just wanted to go home and be happy with my family.

"Ladies line it up, time to go!" Before I knew it we were getting off the elevator. We exited on the basement level and had to walk through a long tunnel to get to court, I felt short of breath and I was full of anxiety and felt faint. It seemed like everything was moving too fast and I just wanted to throw up. The floor began to move and it was moving side to side and I thought I was about to fall. I reached out my hand and I felt the need to hold on to the wall because I thought I was going to fall. As soon as I touched that wall, the staff yelled "Put hands behind your back and lock them now!" I really became nervous then because they didn't understand that I couldn't let the wall go because if I did, I would fall. The staff made everyone stop and grabbed me. I felt like just dropping to the floor till one of the staff said, "She is going to have to go back upstairs." At that moment, I felt something magical come over me called common sense. I knew I didn't want to go back upstairs so my brain went in to auto pilot and straightened me up real quick. I let the staff know that I was feeling much better. I put my hands behind my back and locked them, standing strong and alert like a soldier. We were back on our way and even though I was not feeling well I was able to keep it together till court.

After walking for awhile, we began to see people. For some reason, this made me smile. I felt a sense of calm. I saw the beautiful blue sky and a glimpse of the clouds. The smell of the fresh air brought my anxiety level down. My transformation was almost unbelievable; I didn't have an explanation, I was just glad I felt better. We entered a door that looked like metal bars but we first had to be buzzed in by the sherrif on the other side. Oh my goodness, it was like many areas where the kids were detained. They started to divide us and I was led to a cell where I sat alone with no one to talk to. My thoughts didn't seem like my own. I just

Chapter 5

began to scream for no apparent reason and the sherrif came by the cell and hit on the thick glass sliding door and told me to cut it out or I would be going my ass back upstairs. It seemed like everytime someone mentioned "go back upstairs" I seemed to get it together. So, I sat there staring at the cell and decided to observe the details.

The cell was pretty much like my cell upstairs the brick wall and that disguisting toilet mixed with the sink but the difference was that it was no bed and no desk and the cell was much bigger. The doors were a huge thick glass that slides. I glanced over back to the walls and looked at all the writings on the bricks and then I began to wonder how in the hell did those people get a pen down to court because they really check us thoroughly. There were writing that said Peaches was here and other names as well and I thought, why would anyone want to leave proof that they were in jail? Maybe what they were doing was way above my head because I didn't see a good reason for it.

For some reason, time seemed to be at a standstill. I felt like everything around me seemed to be frozen. After sitting for what felt like hours, I called on my unseen friend. He appeared right away. I began to talk so fast I forgot what I was saying. All I know is that I wanted to go home for the first time in my life. I wanted my mommy but I couldn't shake that dull feeling I had deep down in my gut. My friend didn't reply and I didn't understand why, but that didn't stop me from running off at the mouth. I guess I liked it that way because I had a lot to say. At that moment I was what mattered, because I needed some motivation, I was scared. I saw the sherrif walk towards my cell; I saw her grab the keys off her right side of her hip and momentarily she opened the door and said let's go.

I reacted like I was about to go on stage or something. I felt the most annoying feeling in my butt, my underwear was hiding in my ass. I had to get them out because it just didn't feel right. I made sure the sheriff didn't see me because they may have taken me back upstairs, I didn't want to take any chances. As I walked out of the cell, it was time to put on a smile and look forward to fixing things with my mom.

I entered the courtroom. It looked just like on TV. It was so weird to be in a courtroom as a criminal. The sheriff walked me over in front of the judge and whispered in my ear to put my hands behind my back and don't remove them until she tells me to. I really didn't give a damn because I was that much closer to going home. Immediately, I turned into a big eyed little girl. I couldn't look the judge straight in the eyes because I was scared and besides, he was white. I never really hung around white folks like that unless they were a teacher and of course I was scared of them as well. I'm not sure why, but I guess maybe because their skin color was different. My focus was on the judge when the other guy began to talk. He was saying some pretty bad things about me.

I didn't have a clear understanding of what was going on because they were talking so fast and using words I never heard before. The man next to me began to talk. I began to turn my head, I wanted to see if my mother had come in because I didn't see her when I came into the courtroom , but then I caught myself and remembered the sheriff telling me that I was not to turn around while in front of the judge. It took everything in me to not turn around because I didn't want to find out what the consequences were. Through all the babbling, I heard the judge say, she is to be returned to her mother. Everything inside of me wanted to jump for joy but as I turned around to go back to lock up, I glanced over the court room there was no trace of her.Tears began to roll down my face. I was in there for about two weeks and she never came to see me. That should have been a sign right there. I then ask the

Chapter 5

sherriff that walked me back to the cell was I going home and she said yes, as soon as your mother picks you up. The sherriff noticed that I was crying

"What are you crying for? You're going home."

I told her my mother didn't come I thought she was going to to leave me here. The sherriff replied, "Honey, just because you don't see her in court, don't mean she won't come." This gave me some relief; there was a possibility of my mom picking me up.

I sat in the holding cell until the staff came and picked me up. It seemed as if I waited for hours. I had to wait until everyone was done with their court case. Everyone looked as if they lost their best friend but me. I guess I was going home. The silence was hurting my ears on the way back. I just wanted to talk to distract my thoughts from taking over my emotions.

Finally, we made it back to the tier and we all couldn't wait to talk about what happened at court but we were instructed to go to our rooms because they were about to prepare for lunch.

Time surely went by fast. We left out super early when it was breakfast time and now it's time for lunch. I was okay with chilling in my room for awhile because I had a lot to think about. I had to figure out what would be my first words or would I just run up to her and hug her until my arms to got tired. Although I had a very vivid imagination, it didn't stop me from looking at the positive side of the situation. Before I knew it, I was knocked out asleep. I was awakened minutes later by those loud ass locks on the cell door; it was time to eat lunch and my thoughts brought on a large appetite, I was so hungry I didn't care what it was, I just wanted to eat. I was at the door, ready to to get my eat on and it was sloppy joe day. Now, this was huge. We had some veggie sloppy joe's and of course the milk in the silver pitcher. Everything was so delicous and of course I am exaggerating how good the food was, maybe because I was in a good mood because I was going home. I believe I ate my food so fast that I thought it was good and I never even tasted it. Even after I had eaten all of my food I sat there staring into nowhere ,just stuck. I was trying to find a visual of my mother and I embracing each other and saying things like I love you, but I couldn't gather enough pixels together to make it happen. I decided to watch some TV before my Mom came to pick me up and I found myself smiling because I was finally going home. Then one of the girls said to me "Hey! Aren't you going home today?" And I was like yep and the girl said I can't wait because I go home in three more weeks. My eyes told it all; I felt sorry for her. I don't know why because she didn't seem as though she really gave a damn about herself. We were about the same height but she was a lot skinnier , almost skeleton skinny and she had a tar color skin but very shiney, she had long beautiful hair and the tightest smile. She almost looked like a person from an African war tribe or something.

As she began to talk, for some reason I felt I knew her but I couldn't quite put my finger on it. As she spoke I never payed any attention to what she was saying because I was so focused on where I knew her from. I had to figure this out before she did because it may have been a negative encounter and I had to be prepared to defend myself. I wasn't able to figure out who this girl was. I was kinda mad at myself for not remembering.

I finally asked the girl, "what's your name?"

"Lita King." My mouth immedialty formed the biggest smile ever. It was my friend from the hospital. Remember when good ole mom sent me on vaction for being an habitual runaway? I ran up to her and screamed, "Lita!" She looked puzzeled because she had no clue who I was."Don't you remember Frank and the

Chapter 5

hospital, St. Mary's?" I didn't want to mention the mental issue portion because we didn't need everyone knowing our business.

"She was like, "Lunye, ohhhh. Okay, now I remember you." After she said that, one of the staff asked us both did we want tp go into confinement for the rest of the day. I wanted to say I don't care because I'm going home anyway, but I really didn't want to do the research to find out if I could be detained an extra day because of my behavior , so I was on my way to my cell.

Lita looked as she wanted to keep on talking, but who the hell was she gonna keep talking to? I wasn't go be there on the receiving end and get my ass in trouble. Honestly, I exaggerated our friendship a tad but the truth is, I remembered her but I wasn't like I was best friends with her or anything. I don't know why I dramatized our friendship like that but I knew that this would be beneficial at some point.

When I got in my cell, I just stood there. I put my hands to my face in a prayer position, covering my mouth and trying to get some order in my mind. I paced back and forth to the glass door. And sometimes I would just stand still. I finally sat down on the bed and called on my unseen friend again. It took some time for my friend to arrive, but he eventually appeared and his presence felt quite annoyed. I'm not sure why, but I had plenty of time to get down to it. My first question was, what's wrong? There was no answer, so I figured from his behavior that maybe he was getting tired of me and of course it wouldn't be right if I didn't throw me my own pity party. I began to babble about my mother not being at court and how I had this feeling deep down inside of me that she was going to leave me in that jail. I asked my friend, 'do you think she will come get me?' There was a long moment of silence right up until I heard my number called. In that moment, I felt a sense of relief flow through my body. I knew it was time for me to pack it up and go home. My heart was beating a million times per second, I was so anxious. I was ready to go home to become the perfect child.

My cell door opened and I was there standing pround and excited, I exited the room and I was told to stand under the clock. until a white lady walked through the door. I had a feeling she was there for me, to assist in the process of releasing me to my mom. Again, I felt so anxious. I just wanted to see my mom but the look on the lady's face made my energy level go all the way down. She looked almost like she was annoyed, but also irritated. I was told to go with her and there was no explanation or anything. I just put my hands behind my back and locked as I was instructed. The lady broke the silence as we were walking by asking, "How's it going? I had no words. A response would have been appropriate, but my mind was occupied by who the hell she was and she was walking so damn fast I couldn't breathe, talk and walk fast at the same time. So, I finally responded by saying "Okay." I really wanted to say "Who the hell are you and are you the person that will be processing me out?" But of course, I knew better. We finally made it to an office which delayed the conversation because she pulled out her keys to open the office door and told me to go in and have a seat. It was like any typical office setting, but of couse I couldn't escape the bricks, those damn bricks were everywhere.

She sat down at her desk, I scanned the office briefly before I took a seat. I saw no family pictures; the office was not personalized at all. "My name is Judy Slain, and I am with Child and Family Services."

I didn't understand fully who she was but child and family services sounded good to me because it involved the word family. Maybe she was a counselor for my family when I got home. She grabbed a file off her desk and then the questions began. She

Chapter 5

asked about my mother's contact information and I provided it to her and she asked me when was the last time I talked with my mother. I told her it was before I was locked up and she looked up at me like she was shocked or something, I just wanted to get down to the reason why she wanted to speak to me, why was I in her office? Then she finally came out with it "We have reached out to your mother multiple times today and she has yet to return any calls."

I went silent for a couple of seconds or so and then said, "She be at work at lot and she don't get home till after four p.m."

"Well, we'll give it some time Hon, and see if she returns our calls because we can't house you here after the judge releases you."

I just put my head down in shame. At this point, my hope of going home was just a well thought out plan that didn't look like it was going to happen. Ms Slain then began to ask me about other family members. I had family, but I wasn't sure of their contact information, so I gave her what I thought was my aunt's number and she called and that number was disconnected. Then she looked and me but this time it was with a different look in her eyes almost like she was watching a sad movie or something.

"Are there any other family members you can contact?" For a slight moment I began to daydream and think about family members. I got lost in my thoughts because I was searching my memory for family members and I only knew of a few. I don't really know anyone else's information, my grandma lived in New Orleans and I don't know phone number there, either. Ms. Slain began to wiggle the pen in her hand and bite the end. I sat there patiently and before I knew my mouth flew open and the words, "Am I going home today?" came out.

Run Girl Run!

Before I was able to finish the sentence she interrupted me."I don't know quite yet ,because we haven't talked to your mom yet, once we talk with her, we can go from there."

I instantly felt my eyeballs heat up and the tears were formulating fast. I tried to hold them back by looking up and they still made their presence known because my feelings were hurt. I thought my mother wanted to see me as much I wanted to see her. I thought she missed me because I missed her. I felt the tears roll down my cheek and I turned my head to wipe them away. The counselor observed that I was crying and told me to not worry my mom may be still at work. I looked at the clock; everything in me knew that she was home she just didn't want me home with her anymore. How freakin stupid of me to think that she would want a criminal in her house? Well I guess it was time for me to go back to the tier and all kinds of emotions were going through my head. I couldn't focus because I felt so alone and the anxiety was taking over. I don't even remember the commute back to the tier. All I knew is they were opening the door to let me in. I was told to do the norm like stand under the clock so I could be searched and sent back to my cell. They searched and all I could think about is making it to my cell to get in my bed and cry because crying in front of the girls was not going to happen. I learned that crying in front of the girls was a sign of weakness. I remember seeing the a few of the girls standing in front of their doors looking and me making hand gestures like are about to go home and all I could do is shake my head side to side saying no. After being search I walked to my room really fast because I could feel the tears formulating, I had to get to my safe zone so no one could see me. For the first time the loud sound of the door unlocking sounded like music to my ears. I walked in my cell and flopped on the bed and began to cry silently, the silent cries hurt the most because you have hold back you sound and the sound is what relieves the pressure.

Chapter 5

My head began to hurt because I cried so long, before I knew it the doors were unlocking again it was morning already and I was still there. My breathes became short and my heart was beating really fast and I was looking around as if I was in a strange place, this had to be a nightmare what the hell was going why wasn't I home? Where was my mother. After reality kicked in I realized that I was at the same place I was yesterday which was in a jail cell. Yep you guessed my mother never came to get me.

I had to get back on track and wipe my tears away because I was in jail and no one can see me in weak mode. I had to make sure I had my game face on when I walked the room, so I had to put some cold water on my face to reduce the swelling from my eyes. I've learned that trick good from ole mom. I remember when she would beat me and hit me in the eye, she would tell me to put a piece of ice one my eye to reduce the swelling so she was able to hide the abuse. The sound of the locks clicking startled me because they were so loud. The staff would click the locks several times to let us know that it was time to exit the rooms. It was quite annoying at times but I guess I had to deal with it because I am not staying in a have it your way hotel suite. All of a sudden before I could even recognize the smell of breakfast as I walked out my cell I heard them yell out my last name "Williams" it almost felt like I knew they were going to call my name or something. My heart began to beat really fast because deep down I had a feeling that my mom was going to come she was probably tired that's why she didn't make it yesterday. I walked over to the staff as proud as a wanted to be because deep down I knew that I was going home. The staff stared at me for a moment and looked like she may have thought I had mental issues because I was smiling so hard. Those sweet words were then released out of her mouth "pack it up" I believe the adrenaline was rushing so fast I felt sweat slide down the middle of my back. All of a sudden everything felt like it was going in slow motion. I don't believe I let it all process before I could take off running to my cell seemed like the closer I got to my cell the further it got away.

I eventually made to my cell and for some reason I felt hesitant to leave, it was weird I wanted to leave but I didn't want to leave. For some reason I felt as if I was going to miss being in jail. I believe I was losing my mind or something. I didn't have much to pack but some papers that I wrote on and some notes. All the other stuff I had no use for it. As I took a step towards my freedom I looked back at the cell and stared momentarily and I turned forward and prepared myself to go and be happy.

Well it wouldn't be right unless I stood under that dam clock one more time before I left. The staff didn't even have to tell me this time because I knew the process. I believe I stood there for about fifteen minutes or so but the time move so fast because I was also saying my goodbyes to all the girls and not to mention my mind also was distracted thinking about how my mother's first reaction was going to be when she saw me. I had plans to run up and hug and just hold on to her for many minutes and then we would go home and eat and watch television together. I know it seemed kinda lame but it was my dream. A lady walk through the tier and my thoughts were then paused because I knew she was there to pick me up and walk me down to my mom.

Chapter 6

I was right the lady was there to release me I was instructed to follow her and she was a white lady and she was so pretty and she had on really nice clothing and beautiful blond her pinned up in a bun. I was so happy and nervous all in one. As we exited the tier I put my hands behind my back because that is what I was use to and she stopped and smiled at me and said" sweetie you don't have to lock her hands behind your back now, you are free" I understood what she said but it didn't quite sink in because I unlocked them and after a few steps I locked them again. I'm sure she noticed it but she didn't say anything we just keep on walking. I begin to see the sweet sight of freedom because I was able to see people and the beautiful blue sky through the very large windows in the Audi home.

    I begin to become curious because we began to walk in the parking lot and I don't think you suppose to go to the parking lot to get release. I thought my mom would have had to sign some papers or something. And when the lady walk over to her car everything became clear in that moment. Either she was dropping off at home because my mom was at work or she was taking me somewhere else. After getting into the car with her I couldn't hold it in any longer. "Are you finally taking me home?" She almost seemed as if she didn't want to answer me. She paused for a very long time and then she replied.

"No sweetie. I am taking you to temporary foster placement." The silence filled the air after her response mainly because I didn't understand, I needed time to process the information. After a few minutes or so I realized that she was not taking me home and my last question was why am I going to foster placement and she said "because we have tried to reach out to your mother multiple times and she stated that she did not want you in her home anymore" my eyes began to tear up, I tried everything to hold them back but hurt took over my entire being at that moment. The tears bum rushed my face, I remembered turning towards the window in the car and screaming to the top of my spirit on the inside. I had to talk to my unseen friend immediately because the hurt that I was experiencing I couldn't deal with on my own. But I also knew that I couldn't call my friend in front of the lady because she would have thought I was crazy or something. I remember looking out the window wishing I was dead because I just didn't want to deal with the hurt. The lady at some point said are you okay sweetie and for some reason it felt so sincere and comforting. I wanted to say my feelings are hurt but the tough side of me said I okay, but deep down my emotions were all over the place.

We finally arrive at my temporary foster home and everything in me wanted to just open the door and run because I knew dam well the lady would have tried to chase me and I knew I would have got away but she was to nice and I didn't want to get her in trouble. I sat there as she grabbed her brief case from the back seat and she was rambling through the papers, I'm not sure for what but I became very nervous because I was being placed in a strangers home. She said let's let go and she opened her car door and I just followed with plenty of hesitation. After looking at the house I was beginning to be okay with this foster home thing because the house had a nicely manicured lawn and along the sides were pretty flowers. As we approach the porch I begin to

Chapter 6

think maybe this may turn out to be okay and my thoughts were interrupted by someone coming to the door. It was an older lady she looked about fifty sixty years old her hair was a very dirty gray and she was very short. She had on what looked like a flower nightgown with pockets on the front. She greeted us with a smile and introduced herself. That drew me in because she appeared to be very pleasant. Her name was Mrs. Greene; she was located on the southside of Chicago. I didn't have a clue about the southside of Chicago because I was born and raised on the westside. She opened the door and said "Yall come on in" We walked in her house and I began to scan the place briefly and it was very nice and the furniture had plastic on it and it was so many pictures on the wall, I wondered were those all of her children but the smell of her home I didn't like because it smell like dirty clothing. I began to fall into one my movie thoughts, I was thinking did she only clean up because she knew we were coming? I know I seemed paranoid but my mom made me suspicious of everything because of her behavior.

"What's your name?" I heard Mrs. Greene say in the back of my mind. Somehow, I wasn't able to respond because I was so caught up in my thoughts. She said it again, a little louder. "Lunye."

"That is such a pretty name."

I began to blush and I guessed at this point my life was going to be better off. The social worker looked pleased after she saw me smiling. Mrs Greene took us on a short tour of her home. It was pretty big but it was quite old-fashioned. She showed us where I would be sleeping and it wasn't all that nice but it was much better than what I had which was nothing, so I was grateful. I began to have a slight panic attack once we walked downstairs to the basement.I It smelled musty and it was so dark and gloomy. I heard voices before I could make it to the bottom of the stairs.

It sounded like some young boys and they sounded like they were having a good time but my question was, who are they and why are they here? Before I could ask, Mrs Greene said, "Those are my boys."

Before I could react, we were infront of them. There were four of them and they all looked harmless, but one in particular stood out the most. That one looked kinda weird, weird in a harmless way, but strange. He stood about six one. His face was covered with bumps and his head was shaped like a lemon and his eyes would never stay in one place.

Mrs Greene introduced them all. I didn't say much because I was nervous. They were total strangers and I was the only girl beside Mrs Greene. After speaking to Mrs Greene alone for awhile, the social worker was on her way. I believe in that short time the social worker grew on me because I felt sad when she was leaving. It was almost like she saw the hurt in my eyes because she told me everything is going to be okay , you take care of yourself okay? Then she gave me her card. I watched her leave from the window and all of a sudden Mrs Greene's tone changed.

"I don't allow anyone in my front room. You can either go to your room or you can go and sit on the porch. Even though the words were not harsh, her tone was totally different, it sounded mean and cold. I believe that I overreacted, but I normally can feel a person out on our first encounter. But she was a bit strange, almost like she had multiple personalities. I walked towards the front door and before I knew it, she stopped me again. "You are not allowed to walk out of my front door. You must leave and enter by the back door."

I just rerouted myself to the back door so I can hurry to the front to chill by myself and talk to my unseen friend. I walked around to the front porch. I could hear her boys laughing and

Chapter 6

talking from the basement window. I heard one of them saying she is gonna be my girlfriend and another one said, "I bet Imma get it first."

I thought it was kinda cute because they were checking me out and fussing over me. So, I flopped on the porch and looked up at sky and began to smile momentarily. Then I remembered that I had to talk to my unseen friend about the changes in my life. It took some time for my friend to show up, but eventually he appeared and I was ready to run my mouth like a train on rush hour. I started by sharing that I was out of jail and then went on to tell about my mom not coming to get me and that alone made me began to cry all over again. I then began to vent about being sent to a foster home. My friend was not very responsive, but who cares? At this point, all I wanted was for someone to listen to me.

I heard someone say "Hey girl, my mother said come here."

I looked to my right; it was one of her sons calling me. I didn't verbally respond, I just got up and walked towards the back and followed him in the house. I wasn't ready to go in and talk with her. I wanted to enjoy the beautiful weather being that I was locked up all that time. A few weeks can take a toll on a kid in jail.

All at once she blurted out. "You will respond to me, yes ma'am and no ma'am, is that understood?"

"Yes ma'am."

"You have to earn your keep around here. Nothing in life is free"

I knew for sure at that moment that this lady was a fraud. I wasn't even in her home a good hour before she told me I needed to clean the kitchen. I didn't have much of a choice, so I did what she demanded. She had the nerve to sit in the kitchen and watch me while she sat on the phone with one of her friends talking loud as ever and using more profanity than regular words.

Tears formed in my eyes and I just let them fall. She was not able to see them anyway, because my back was to her and she was too busy gossiping any way. I just wanted to walk out the door and never look back. But I didn't have anywhere to go and I didn't want to be on the streets, so I had to just deal with it. As long as I wasn't physically abused, I was all good. I finished the kitchen I must have done a good job because there were no complaints. I decided to go to my sleeping quarters to relax for a little. The room that she gave me looked like it was for a single old man. The smell was a mixture of dirty laundry and air freshner. The wallpaper was very old but it was holding up. I flopped on the bed and just sat thinking I should be grateful. However, an inner part of me that wanted to just get up and leave. I was in that room literally twenty minutes before I heard a knock at the door. It was her again, asking me if I knew how to wash clothing. I knew that she wanted me to do laundry, so I said no. "Come come on down to the basement so I can teach you how to wash because you are too damn old not to know how."

Oh my goodness I wanted to tell her fuck you I don't feel like doing shit, but deep down inside I knew that it would not end up good at all, so I humbled myself and walked as slowly as I could. "Hey, young lady, you need to put some pep in your step!"

All I could do was roll my eyes and continue to make my way to the basement. I began to slide my hand on every wall that I walked by; sorta like marking my territory. I finally made it to the basement and she told me,' we are going to start by separating the clothing.'

In the back of my head I was like, I know how to do this but I had to pretend like I was really paying attention because if I

Chapter 6

let on that I knew how to do this she would know I lied. As she was talking, I just kept nodding my head as if I was really paying attention. I was thinking about making a run for it, but a voice inside my head kept informing me I had nowhere to go. I quickly put my thoughts on hold because I heard the lady in the back of my thoughts asking me, 'do you understand?'

"Yes, ma'am."

"I am about to go upstairs and get the rest the clothes."

In the back of my mind I was like, damn, there's more. I wonder if she saving these clothes so she could have someone like myself to come over to slave for her. By the time she came back down, I had separated all the clothing and was ready to load the washer.

"Good job, you learn fast. I am going to teach you a lot things because you can't live in someone's house for free; you have to earn your keep."

I just looked at her with disappointment because she thought I was just plain ole stupid. I guess after she figured I had the hang of everything, she left me alone to wash about seven loads or so. I really didn't care, I just wanted her to shut up and get out of my face. She finally left my sight and went upstairs. I was pissed because I was being treated like a damn slave. The crazy part of it all is she had sons that could have done this shit. I began kicking and stomping on the their stanking ass clothing to relieve some frustration, then a few minutes later came the tears, thinking about my mom. I was just wondering what was she doing right at that moment. I guess I missed her, but I didn't miss the ass beating. Before I knew it, I heard the washing machine buzz that was the indicator that the machine was done washing. I grabbed the clothing out of the washing machine and put them in the dryer and prepared the next load. I paused for a second because I heard someone coming. Whoever it was sounded like they were tip toeing. So I stood still, so I could figure out the direction the sound was coming from. The sound came closer and closer "Who is it?" All of a sudden, her oldest son came from around the corner looking creepy as ever. I broke the two minute silence by saying, 'your momma went upstairs.'

"I know."

In my head I was like, what the hell you standing here for unless he wanted to finish up washing their funky ass clothes? I was getting irritated and he also maded me feel uncomfortable. I just began to finish up putting the laudry in the washer but I was watching his ass like a hawk from my side view. He stared at me for a long time with nothing to say and then he finally walked away towards the back door of the basement. *Phewww*! I was so damn happy his creepy ass left; now I could relax. I leaned on the washer with both elbows and thought about getting the hell out of that house and where the hell would I go. I got scared when the washer started to tumble because it was so loud. I then began to sort out more loads because I wanted to have the next load prepared. As I was preparing the load, I saw something that looked like money. Oh my goodness, my heart was beating so fast. I looked around to make sure that no one was looking and then I moved a few clothing items and there sat a fifty dollar bill. Everything in me wanted to scream out loud with joy but I couldn't do that. I grabbed the money so fast I didn't even see my hands move. Deep down, I knew it was wrong to keep the money but the immediate part of my brain was in control. I stashed the bill in my panties. I have no clue why I chose to put it there but it was an automatic thing, I guess. I was happy; My thoughts were moving so fast I forgot what I was thinking. I had to take moment and figure out my next move, because this could have been a

Chapter 6

setup to see if I was going to give the money back. I began to pace back and forth, looking around as if someone was watching me. Then I stopped and my focus turned to the couch in the sitting area. I rushed over to the couch and took the fifty dollars out of my panties and stuffed it in the sides of the couch. I belived it was a good idea because if it was a trap and if the lady wanted to search me, the money would not be on me. Yep I was ready for whatever because I was going to use that fifty dollars to get the hell out of there. I immediately went back to washing their clothing and time went past so fast I didn't even noticed it was getting dark. I only had two loads left and I kept my eye on the stairs leading to the first floor of the house. As soon as I began to relax, I heard the sound of someone two stepping down the stairs. Oh my goodness, I began to sweat. I had so many thoughts within those couple of seconds. I was going to run by the couch and get the fifthy dollars and just give it to Mrs Greene, but I decided to just try my luck. Before I knew it, there she was, standing there as ugly as she wanted to be, with her hands on her hips. She didn't say anything for awhile. I just started to act like I was busy moving clothes around.

"I see you are almost done. I guess I will finish up and you can go take a bath and get yourself prepared for bed. I looked at her with disappointment because I wasn't ready to leave. My damn money was in the couch and I wasn't able to get it. I walked upstairs in slow motion looking back at the couch as if it was my best friend. I made it up the stairs to the first floor and I began to kick and punch at the air. I was interrupted by one of her sons walking in the front door He looked at me like I was crazy, but he didn't say anything and I didn't say anything. I thought to myself, I hope he don't say anything to his mom about my actions. I then made my way to my assigned room. I flopped on the bed and just sat there.How the hell was I going to be able to get the money out of the couch? I would worry about that later I had to make plans to get the hell out of there.

I was thinking maybe I can make a run for it on the weekend, like Friday or Saturday. That meant I had two more days to come up with a plan. I made my way to the bathroom and realized in that moment I had no clothing to change into, so I ran the water in the tub and locked the door and I decided that I would fake taking a bath. I sat on the end of the tub and swung my hand back and forth in the water to make sound like I was bathing. After fifteen minutes or so, I threw a little water in my face and walked out the bathroom, not even realizing duh I still had on my clothing , but thank goodness no one was nearby.

I went into my room and laid down with my back on the bed and my feet on the floor. For awhile, I just laid there, looking at the ceiling and before you know it, I was sound asleep. When I woke up it was still dark. I looked over at the clock; it was 2:38am. I stretched and looked around and a sporadic thought came to me. Everyone in the house should be asleep so maybe I should make my way to the basement and get my fifty dollars. Well of course it's not rightfully mine, but finders keepers losers weepers. I peeked out of the room to make sure the coast was clear. I didn't hear a sound but the sound of the air conditioner and the sound of the smoke detector beeping simultaneously. I walked out of the room, making my way to the stairs and all of a sudden I made a loud sound. I believe it came from the floor creaking or something. I stood there for about thirty seconds to see if anyone else heard. I was ready to run tip toe back to the room. Well, it seemed no one heard so I crept down the stairs. It almost felt like I was in a scary movie

I made it down to the first floor and I was getting close. As soon as I made to the basement door and as soon I did, a loud

Chapter 6

sound from the door opening scared the hell out of me. I looked around and the coast was clear, so I went down the basement stairs very carefully. I was sweating like a slave. I made it down the stairs and I heard some rap music. It concerned me because everyone should have been asleep so I figured someone may have left the music on by accident. I made my way down the rest of the stairs and I was so happy because there it was, the couch that I put the crispy fifty in. All I could do was smile as I walked towards the couch. My thoughts were interrupted by Mrs Greene's oldest son, standing by the television with his hands in his shorts. I was disgusted and I felt like a deer in headlights. I didn't know what to do or say, so I immediately walked over by the washing machine as if I was checking the laundry but there was no laundry because Mrs. Greene had finished it.. Now I was getting scared. I walked toward the stairs to make my way back to my room and I felt him behind me. He broke the silence by saying come here. I wanted to run, but my legs wouldn't move. So I turned around and said why?

"Just come here for a second, I want to ask you something." I turned around slowly and walked towards him. I stopped a few steps away from him and he asked me how old I was. I told him I was thirteen. He kept licking the bottom of his lip and said, 'I like you.'

I began to feel that feeling in my stomach , you know the pervert alert. I didn't kow what to say in that moment and he had the nerve to walk towards me and kiss me. I was scared and angry at the same damn time. I snatched away from him and he grabbed my hand and pulled me towards him. I yelled stop and he let me go. I ran upstairs so fast I couldn't feel my feet.

Mrs Greene yelled, "Who is that?"

I didn't say a word I just closed my door and laid in the bed. I cried all that night. I wanted to leave as soon as possible, but

Run Girl Run!

I couldn't until I got the money out of the couch. I was not able to sleep at all. I watched that door all night till morning came. I was so tired I didn't care. I got up and it was about 7am in the morning and I walked to the door and put my ear next to it to see if the coast was clear. Everything was pretty quiet for the moment. So, I opened the door slowly and walked casually down the stairs. I paused when I made it to the first floor; I wanted to listen for any signs of those boys. Everything seemed quiet, so I then tiptoed down to the basement. I stood at the bottom of the stairs for about fifteen seconds to scan the area and make sure coast was clear. I moved quickly over to the couch and sat down because I had to make sure I wasn't caught. After a few seconds or so, I stuck my hand in the pot of gold, sorry, I mean the couch and got my nifty fifty. I immediately stuffed in my panties and sat still for a few seconds and looked around to make sure everything was clear. I got up and ran up those stairs so fast you would have thought lightning pierced my tail. I made it past the first floor. Now all I had to do is make it to the top floor where my room was.I It wasn't easy because everyone was awake. It had me wondering why all of a sudden. It was quite early but I had to make it to my room without looking suspicious. I grabbed the railing of the staircase and I took them two at a time. That was a bad idea because it had been awhile since I did that and it stretched all kind of muscles in my legs. I made it to the top of the stairs and I paused for a moment and I heard the most annoying t.v show theme song from the *Andy Griffith* show. Oh my goodness, the whistling made me just want to scream. I just tried to block it out much as I could and made my way to my room. The sweet sound of success was the squeaky sound of my door opening. I closed it sofly and sat on my bed and laid back. Moments later, I dug in my panties to get the money. I held it in both my hands and smiled at it. I even smelled it and it smelled like money normally smells. I guess I was looking for a sour smell

Chapter 6

on the money because I haven't bath since I got out of jail. I am just telling the truth!

Then I heard the floor creak outside of my door; someone was coming. I had to hide the money quick. I couldn't risk getting caught. I heard Mrs. Greene yelling by my door "Yall come out here for a second." I quickly put the money back into my panties just in case. I walked out of the room and I felt a weird feeling because everyone was standing in the hall. Mrs Greene didn't look too happy either. I walked towards everyone with a concerned look on my face. She yelled for her oldest son. She began to talk and she souned rather angry but she spoke softly "Did any of y'all see fifty dollars?" I immediately broke out in a sweat and all of my muscles in my body tensed I wanted to scream and run at the same time. Before I could reply, she turned her old worn out eyes towards me and said "Did you see any money while you were washing because I may have left it in my back pocket of those jeans I had on."

I quickly responded no. There were beads of sweat on my upper lip.

"What did you just say to me?

"No, ma'am I saw her shoulders relax. That was the error. I can't believe I can just lie that easy and have no remorse. Her sons all said the same thing and I stood there as she insulted them for about three minutes, saying, they were only good for stealing from her and this wouldn't be the first time. I just stood there as if I didn't have a care in the world. Well. I was rather irritated because I had to listen to her talk and threaten us if she finds out we did it or not. I didn't give two shits because I was leaving anyway. She finished off by saying, 'y'all can get the hell out of my face because if I catch one of y'all lying I'm beating my kids ass and you, young lady will be getting the hell up outta here."

Run Girl Run!

Mrs Greene's oldest son walked off first and I made sure I was the last to leave, just in case she wanted to fuss some more. She actually walked off before I did.

I went back to my room and stood with my back facing the door just standing there it as if someone was trying to get in. Finally, I flopped back on the bed. I needed to come with an escape plan fast. I stood up and looked out the window and knew there was no way I would jump because one, I was scared and two, I knew I couldn't escape if my body was injured. I took the money out of my panties again and put it inside of one of the coats I saw in the closet. I was going to make my move soon, so I schedualed a bath in my head because I couldn't go out funky. I went to ask Mrs Greene for something I could put on after my bath and she gave me some of the ugliest worn out clothing she could find.

"When yo case worker get you a voucher, we can go up to Sears and get you some things."

I really didn't give a shit. I was going to wash my clothing and then make my move anyway. I went to the bathroom and scrubbed my body down as if it was going to be my last bath. I must say they had plenty of bath soap and bubble bath. The whole time I was in the tub I was thinking about my escape. Then I remembered the money. What if someone walks in there and finds it? I rinsed the soap fast and put on the clothing Mrs Greene gave me, they were all itchy and hanging off of me. My shoulder was exposed like a glazed pork chop. The skirt she gave me looked wool, it was gray and plaid with pleats on it and it was long and uneven on me. I cleaned the tub and I gathered all my clothes and made my way to my room. Okay, now it was time to put my clothes in the washer. I felt myself formulating a smile because the time was near and I had to go back to my room because I didn't feel comfortable with the money being left there. I ran back to my room and I got

Chapter 6

my cash. I forgot I had no panties to put my money in because I had no panties to put on. I was basically going commando with a damn skirt on, I felt so uncomfortable but I had to do what I had to do because I was not putting on no dirty panties. I just put the money back in the coat and made my way back to the basement so I could wash my clothing. I made it down stairs to the basement and I walked straight over to the washer and put my clothing in there and added a lot of detergent because they were really dirty. I felt really bogus so I made my way back to the stairs to get back to my room and make plans to leave. I think I was gonna make break tomorrow because tomorrow was Friday and the weekend is always the time to run. As I was about to run up the stairs, Mrs Greene's oldest son stopped me at the stairs,

"Come here, girl."

"No!" I began making my way up the stairs, he grabbed me and put his hand under my skirt and I snatched away from him and ran. I was so disgusted I almost fell up the stairs. I slammed the door when I got to the first floor and ran up to my room, fast, but quietly. What the fuck am I going to do? I paced the floor, back and forth, back and forth. I finally sat down and threw up. It wasn't a lot, but it was enough to clean up. I felt disgusting, I wanted to scream; I wanted out right now. I grabbed the middle of the skirt I had on and gathered the front and back part of the skirt and pinned it together so that my vagina would not be exposed. I stood up again and paced the floor again. I was debating should I go tell or not, but I'm sure she wouldn't believe me because that was her son. So, I just waited patiently because there was no way in hell I was staying another day after that. I was sure the washer had stopped by now and I needed to put my clothes in the dryer. I was scared to go back to the basement because I'm sure he would have tried something and maybe even succeeded. I had to think of something fast. As soon as I said that, I came up with a plan.

I went to the hall area on the top floor and yelled Mrs Greene's name. She responded fast. I asked her could she show me how to start the dryer? "What do you need to dry?"

"My clothes."

"I know you didn't put just those few clothes in my washing machine." I just stood there looking stupid.

"Get that shit out of my washer and hang that shit in front of the fan."

I didn't really care at that moment as long as she accompanied me to the basement and she did just that. We made it to the basement and there was no sign of her son and that was cool with me too. I got my clothes and took them up to my room and I blocked out everything she was saying because I was focusing on my great escape. I walked in my room and put the clothes on the bed so I could pop the wrinkles out of them. The wet clothes made a wet stain on my bed, but I didn't care because I was leaving anyway. I saw a fan by the closet and I got it and plugged it up and it was so much dust coming from that fan it triggered my allergies. I had to deal with it for a moment so I could dry my clothes. As I sat there, patiently waiting on my clothes to dry, I tried to feel bad for stealing the money but I couldn't. It's almost like she deserved it or something. Before you knew it, two hours past and my clothing was still damp. I knew it might feel a little uncorfortable but I put them on damp because I had to go. At least my panties were a little dryer than everything else. So, I was dressed and ready to get gone. I was so damn nervous, I hope they didn't try to chase me down or something. Maybe I was overthinking things, I just got up and walked out my room and jogged down the stairs as if I was an adult or something and walked out the front door and I was on my way and then I realized the money was in the room in the coat.

Chapter 7

Oh my goodness, I felt so stupid. I had to go back up the stairs and get the money and the killer was I barged out the front door. I humbled myself because I needed the money. I walked back in and to my surprise no one was in plain sight or even noticed that I left out the front door. I hurried up to the room and got the money and made my way back out the door. I was finally gone. I went from nervous to happy as hell. I had fifty dollars and I was out of that hell hole. I didn't feel a bit of resentment I just wanted out.

I was a bit hungry but it wasn't a good idea to stop at anything local because they might be looking for me sooner than I thought. I stopped at the gas station to get some change, so I grabbed a few bags of chips and a strawberry pop. The man gave me my change and I was on my way. As soon as I walked out of the store, a bus was coming. Yes! Right on time! I got me a transfer and sat down with relief. The ride was bumpy because I sat in the back of the bus. I was on my way to nowhere. I didn't know where I was going but I was going. I believe I enjoyed the ride so much I fell asleep and in just that little time, had a nightmare of that disgusting son of Mrs Grene. I hated him for what he did to me, it brought back so many memories I just wanted to go away. I woke up and I thought I woke on my own but the bus driver had been calling me for the last ten minutes. He said he didn't want to come by me because I was acting kinda weird. What he didn't know is that I was having a nightmare.

"You better hurry up and leave because I called the police."

I took off so fast; I couldn't take a chance on the police catching up to me because I am sure they had reported me missing by now. I found myself crying because it was getting dark and I was getting scared because bad things always happen when it's dark. I called on my unseen friend and he didn't show up. I didn't understand why because everything seemed good that last time I spoke to him. I had to find somewhere to go while it was still before curfew. I saw a pay phone and called my crush slash future husband. Thank God he answer the phone. I said, can I speak to "Devin"

"That's me." he said, even though I knew it was him. We chatted for a brief moment and I interrupted the conversation by saying I wanted to stop by. He didnt hesitate by saying no, so I was on my way. He didn't know that I was considered a runaway and I wasn't gonna tell him either. I was thinking hard and long about what I was going to say and how the hell was I going to get him to say yes to me spending the night. The ride was long, but that gave me some time to think of a lie.

The next stop was my stop and I had that nervous feeling because I hadn't seen him a while. I pulled the cord down to let the bus driver know I wanted to get off. I fixed my hair the best I could while looking in the window of the bus because I was able to see my reflection. The bus stopped and I walked to the the door and made my way off the bus. I almost forgot I needed some gum to freshen up my breath so I stopped at the corner store and brought me some Doublemint. Yes I was sure this would get the job done. I was two blocks from his house and I was walking slow as ever, like I had all the time in the world. It felt quite good

Chapter 7

walking down his block because I could just feel his presence, like a pot of gold at the end of the rainbow. I was finally in the front of his house, it was huge and beautiful. I wished for that moment it was his and my house. Then reality kicked in when I heard that damn bee by my ear. I walked to the side of his house and rang the bell and his mom came to the door. "Is Devin here?" She called his name really loud and he let me in and I walked down to the basement and I heard his mom say, don't be having company late and he was like okay mom and he through his hand up in the air like he was saying watever behind her back. I walked in; it was just like I like it, nice and clean. I toyed around most of the time like he wasn't the reason I was there but I'm sure he knew otherwise because I didn't leave. Okay, I believe the hard to get thing was irritating him so I decided to bring up this girl we went to school with. Her name is Latasha and the only reason I brought it up because I saw them on a picture together and his response was she is just cool with me. Everything in me knew he was probably lying but it felt better to believe what he said.

Even if he was lying, I still was drawn to him. I'd never felt this type of feeling before. The strangest sense of desire came upon me. I felt my petunia pulsating and I wanted him to kiss me more than I'd ever wanted anything. I had to figure out a way to toy with him to draw him closer to me. So, I pretended to want to leave because of the other girl; I thought that would make him want to stop me from leaving, and he would chase after me instead. And guess what? I was right.

As I was walking towards the door, he ran up behind me and grabbed me from behind. Oh my goodness, it made me feel so good inside. He guided my body toward his room. I faked resisting him until finally we made it to his room. It was so dark we couldn't see each other. He began to rub on my body; it felt so good, but my brain was telling me to stop this nonsense and get the hell up out of there because I didn't really know anything about having sex. The only experience I had was being raped and these feelings felt nothing like that. I just didn't care; I wanted to give myself to him because I didn't want him to have sex with anyone else. I was very scared but very ready to get this sex thing over with. I knew the basics, I just didn't have a clue about making the choice on your own. For once in my life, I was very much in control.

I must have felt confident because I was kissing him like I was experienced. It came naturally because I was really feeling him. I thought I would finally have someone that would be mine and who would love me forever. My body rubbed up against his and I felt his erection, and became extremely nervous because it was a little more than I expected. I had so many conflicting thoughts in that moment. I wanted to just walk out , but there were so many reasons I found to stay. That's when I added to my suffering. I'm not saying he treated me bad but the truth was a stranger to him. I never told him everything that was going on in my life and he never told me his true intentions when it came to me. All I can remember is that my first experience was all based on a feeling that invaded my body without warning. I wanted to be loved and a part of something so bad that I gave my virginity away without even weighing the consequences. The whole time I wanted to stop because it was painful and it made me have flash backs of being raped but I never told him to stop. I felt it was too late, that if I stopped he wouldn't like me anymore. I had no knowledge of condoms or any type of sex education, for that matter. I was just a young girl looking for love and giving up what I thought would make him stay with me forever. A few minutes into my first consensual encounter I felt like a victim and I didn't understand why. So I blanked out mentally until I felt him flop on me and began to breathe as if he just got through running a marathon. Oh my goodness! He was so sweaty and sticky I just wanted to scream

Chapter 7

and run but I was able to train myself to act like it was a great experience and put my clothing on and just leave. He wanted to talk and I didn't, for some reason ,I felt gross and I just wanted to take a bath but I remembered I don't have a home to go to.

Damn what am I going to do? I asked him if I could use his bathroom and he showed me where it was, I went in there and squatted down and silently screamed. I rubbed my ear against my shoulder and closed my eyes, hoping this was all just a bad nightmare. I looked around for some clean towels because I was going to wash up and just throw the towel away. I know throwing the towel away was stupid but I didn't want him knowing that I washed up. I was going to do a fast and quick wash and no one would know a thing. I didn't see a clean towel in sight so I did what I thought would work. I was gonna wash up with some paper towels and soap until he said I have to use the bathroom, Now this ruined all my plans so I had to fake like I just peed and flush the toilet. As I was fixing my pants I felt something wet coming out of me, now I'm thinking I'd gotten my period, so now I'm embarrassed and had to move fast. I quickly grabbed a lot of tissue and rolled up like a pad and put it in my underwear. I didn't like the way that felt and looked at the shower. I just wanted to get in the shower and wash my ass but I was so young and stupid I thought that it was embarrassing to ask. So I looked at myself one more time in the mirror and made my way out of the bathroom. He looked irritated when I came out. He was probably thinking that I took a crap in his bathroom , that's me, always coming with a thought for everyone. It was just something I did randomly, I don't have a clue why I did it but it always seemed to be negative. I tried walking sexy to keep him attracted to me, I felt so lame for all the extra but I couldn't change what was already done. He walked in the bathroom and closed the door but looked back at me with a slight smile. Now that kinda settled my nerves somewhat but my focus immediately turned towards the uncomfortable feeling from the tissue in my panties. I had to get out of there a.s.a.p, so I had to think of something fast. When he came out the bathroom I started acting as if time was passing me by too fast. I told him I was late for curfew. I walked past him, bouncing slowly from hip to hip with a side smirk to play cool. For some reason, that walk to the door felt like forever. I really wanted to spend the night but there was no way I was asking him because then he would know I was a runaway and that meant the other girl wins. It was so weird how my emotions just switched up so fast from wanting to go and not wanting to go, then needing to go.

He hugged me and I felt that mushy feeling again, almost like love. He turned me around and I remember smiling on the inside and being fisty on the outside. When he kissed me, it lasted for about thirty seconds or so. But as soon as I walked out the door I began to cry like crazy. I felt like he'd betrayed me. I hated him; I wanted him to stop me and tell me to stay with him but he let me just walk out that door in the dark to be scared. All I could do is walk and cry.

After a few minutes, I remembered him saying call him when I got home. After walking for about an hour or so, my thoughts switched to cleaning my tail. My first idea was to go to Mickey D's and use the bathroom sink. I walked a block or so and I was so damn happy to see Mickey D's I wanted to scream. I walked in and stood in the long line like I was about to buy something. I stood there for a couple of seconds and then asked for the key to the bathroom. Just as I thought, she gave me the key with no problem. Thank goodness it was a single bathroom but I still knew I had to hurry before somebody else needed to use it. I grabbed a few paper towels and began to take care of my hygiene. I was almost sure that I felt my period coming down but I didn't see any blood so I utilized those paper towels to the best of my ability.

Chapter 7

I made it the counter and gave the cashier the key back. I even decided to stand back in line and order some food. My all-time favorite, the mighty Big Mac with fries. As I stood there, I began to think about Devin but I didn't feel the connection I'd felt when I was with him. Hmmmmm! I was next in line and I was hungry. I got my food and anxiously opened my bag, walking out the door and gobbling those hot ass fries. I didn't care because I was hungry. Before I knew it, I had walked about four blocks or so. This guy and his cousins were on a porch and he yelled out, "Can I walk with you?"

I turned and looked at him; he was so cute and I was alone. "If you want to," I said. I purposely slowed down so he could catch up to me and he did. He asked me my name and I told him Ne-Ne. He said his was David. We walked and talked and talked and walked for over an hour and we were only walking in circles. He finally told me to sit on his porch until he came back from the bathroom. He went up the stairs. I knew I had nowhere to go, so I was thinking, maybe I could just hang out with him as long as I could and then think about my next location.

My thoughts were interrupted by the loud sound of his door. He walked out moments after the door opened.

"Are you cool? He asked.

"Yeah," I told him. "I'm good." It was a real now moment. We sat on his porch and talked all night. Well, it wasn't exactly his porch, it was his grandma's porch. I felt so comfortable with him and I'd only just met him. He seemed quite curious as to why I was out so late, but I am glad he never asked because I would've had to come up with a lie. He did ask if I had somewhere to go and I lied and said yes. I told him my aunt was gone out of town until Friday, but I locked my keys in the house. It was Monday, so that meant I was homeless in his eyes for four days. He paused for a moment and he looked as if he wanted to ask me another question but he didn't; he just told me that he would be right back. I sat on the stump on this porch with my legs swinging side to side and in that moment wondered about my mother. Was she thinking about me, did they call her yet and let her know that I was missing? Well, I tried very hard to get those thoughts out of my head because they were making my heart beat really fast. I couldn't get her out of my head, so I began to shake my head really fast as if my thoughts would just fall out of my ear or something. I heard a noise and for a moment I forgot where I was and who I was with, so when David walked out the door I was startled for a moment. But at Least I wasn't thinking about my mother anymore.

He had some food. I wasn't really hungry but if he offered me some I wasn't gonna turn it down. And just like the gentleman he was, he offered me some of his food. I didn't want to look greedy. I swear, there are so many rules dealing with guys, I just wanted to be me. I watched him as he ate his food and I wanted some so bad because he had some pot roast, baked mac and cheese and some yams. He said his grandmother cooked and this was something she did on the regular. I wanted some so bad even though I just ate some Mickey D's a couple of hours ago. He was babbling on about why he was staying with his grandmother, but to be honest, I didn't care, I needed somewhere to stay for the night. You would think I would be scared, but I wasn't. I was more scared of being on the streets.

We were interrupted by some loud voices approaching us. It was about four young girls, like myself. We both got quiet and David began to smile as if he knew them. All of a sudden, they walked up on the porch. In that millisecond, I had so many thoughts and they all ended with me fighting somebody. Then he said, "Ne-Ne these are my cousins."

Chapter 7

What a relief. I was able to exhale and let my guard down. So he introduced everyone and they seemed pretty friendly. One of his cousins blurted out, "Let's go down to my house and kick it on the porch."

David looked at me silently, as if he was asking me a question. I just looked at him like he was crazy. "Then he said, "You want to go down the street?"

I wanted to say no but I just said yes because I thought that's what everyone wanted me to say. And there we were, on our way to the next location. I was hoping it wasn't a long walk because I was tired. Lucky me, we only walked a block. We found us a seat on the porch and sat still for a moment and just listened to the night air and the sounds of cars driving past. I slapped my arm, a damn bug was biting me. The sound of that arm slap made everyone look at me and I just looked at them back. Finally, David broke the ice by saying he was about to fight some dudes earlier. I really could care less because I had my own issues to deal with. It was getting really late and his cousins began to go in, one at a time. Before you knew it, it was just me and him, looking at the stars. He moved to the couch that was on the porch and he sat there for about three minutes or so and asked me to sit next to him and of course I got up and made my way to him. Before you knew it, we both fell asleep.

It was morning and I didn't have a clue what time it was. The birds were chirping and the freshness of the morning air let me know it was very early. David was still asleep, and I had so many thoughts in my head I felt faint. I stayed in the same position for as long as I could; then I just leaned forward to gather my thoughts and nudged him a few times to wake him up. He looked at me of course, like who the hell are you? But just for a moment. Then he smiled and stretched at the same time.

"Damn! I don't even remember falling asleep."

"Me either." I still didn't have a clue to where I was going but I had to play it off and go somewhere, so I didn't look too thirsty. So I told him I was leaving and began walking down the stairs and he stopped me.

"Where are you going?"

"To my aunt's house to get cleaned up." I knew I was lying, but he didn't. He told me to take his number and call him later so we could kick it. That worked for me because I didn't have shit else to do. He asked for a hug and I was so happy on the inside my armpits began to sweat. I believe I was more grateful that someone showed they cared about me. I was on my way again this time, knowing that I have somewhere to come back to.

That one night turned into a forced love affair. I was in need of a place to stay and food to eat. David couldn't get enough of me. I totally blocked out Devin as if he never existed. I spent most of my time with David; he was the one that was available, he was the one that made sure that I had a place to stay.

Months later, that sweet David turned into someone else. He starting hitting me and calling me names. I felt obligated to him because of my circumstances. I had become good friends with the family and I would spend nights with him at his grandmother's house. Sometimes I would stay nights at his cousins' house. Either way, I always had somewhere to sleep until one day his cousin told me he had another girlfriend. I was sick to my stomach, I wanted to scream and become violent in that moment but I keep my cool because his cousin made me swear I wouldn't say anything. So, I secretly tried everything to fix it but there was something about this girl he was drawn to. Whenever I could, I cried. I felt betrayed but I didn't know what to do. I knew it was because I was always

Chapter 7

there and he knew I was a runaway. Maybe I shouldn't have let him know about what was going on with my mother. I felt so alone; there was nothing I could do or say to fix it. I hated myself. I just wanted to turn myself in and just deal with any consequences.

One day, I was sitting on the porch. It was beautiful weather and I smelled some barbeque. It smelled so good I wanted to find out who was cooking and ask for a piece. I saw David walking down the street with a bag and he looked excited, so that put me at ease. He walked right past me and didn't say anything. I wanted to say something but my pride wouldn't let me. Hours passed before I went into the house and I noticed that he'd put on new clothes, so that's what was in the bag. *Hmmmmm* I believe it's about time for me to say something.

"Where you going? I asked. He didn't say anything, he just kept getting dressed. I stood leaning on the wall watching him, wanting to just kill him. After he got done getting dressed, he skipped down the stairs and stood on the porch, looking just as fine as he wanted to be. I stood there in the doorway.

"Where are you gonna go?"

"With my girlfriend." He didn't even look at me.

Everything in and on my body shut down. I could not believe he said that to me. I was his girlfriend, why was he saying this to me. I began to cry immediately and all I could say was I hate you. He didn't show any emotion, he just stood there as if he didn't say what he said.

A car drove up, it was one of his buddies. He skipped down the stairs and didn't look back. I cried and I cried. I couldn't sleep. That whole night, I went to the porch for an hour, came back upstairs and went back to the porch until it was 5:30 a.m. I was so tired but my feelings drowned all that out. I just wanted him to come in.

I was going to tell him I loved him and I was sorry. I had no clue why I was going to tell him I was sorry; I was just going to do whatever to get my man back. He never came back that night. I didn't see him until 5p.m. the next day and he was with a girl. I was so devastated, I wanted to fight and I didn't even care if I won or not.

Before he could walk on the porch, I walked off the porch with hurt in my eyes. His eyes met mine but he didn't even care. I walked away, fast and angry, with all type of hate in my heart. Even so, I wanted him to run after me and say he was sorry. I ended up walking like, five blocks before I figured out he wasn't coming after me. My life was over. I cried so hard and so long I became weak. I'd made up in my mind I wasn't going back because I was hurt and embarrassed. I mean there was no reason to go back. I went to the liquor store because I needed a drink. I wasn't old enough to buy it so I did what all teenagers do, ask a wine head and give him a buck. I got me some white port and kool aid and a forty ounce of eight ball beer. I walked and drank and walked and drank. I was so drunk all I could do was cry and think about how my mother didn't want me and David didn't want me. I felt like I wasn't supposed to be born because nothing good ever happened to me. I wanted to end it all. I thought if I killed myself maybe it would make everyone feel bad for hurting me. I had to use the bathroom and I had to think quickly. I was not far from this girl that does hair so I made my way over to her house and knocked on her door and no one came. As I was stumbling down the stairs, a lady came to the door and said can I help you?

"Is Helen home?" She said no. I said thank you and I continued to walk away. I was kinda moving side to side because I had to pee and number two.

"Are you okay?" I told her I had to use the bathroom and she said come on in baby and use the restroom. I still felt numb but I had strength enough to make my way to the bathroom. She

Chapter 7

walked in the house first and pointed the way. Thank goodness, it was clean. I put some tissue on the toilet and flopped my butt on that toilet and released all that pressure. I know I was bogus for taking a shit but I had to go. Now I was done and I had to clean my tail with some wet tissues and wash my hands. After I washed my hands I looked around for the air freshener to get rid of the smell but I didn't see any, so I opened the medicine cabinet and all I saw was pills and toothpaste. I grabbed one bottle of the pills without even looking to see what they were. Even if I did I wouldn't have understood what they were for anyway. I had plans on ending it all because I didn't feel worthy of life. I stuffed the pills in my pants and poured some pine sol in the toilet and flushed to help get rid of the smell.

I looked at myself in the mirror one time before I left. My eyes were red as hell and I was so ugly. I exited the bathroom and told the lady thank you and made my way back to the streets. I began crying again and I went back to the store to get some more beer because that's all I could afford. I walked to the alley, feeling sorry for myself and called my unseen friend. He wouldn't respond, so I made my way halfway down the alley and leaned back on one of those big garbage dumpsters and began to cry some more. I hated the smell of the garbage can, but I had my mind made up; I was gonna end it all. I felt the nasty grit on the ground as I sat down, drunk and hurt. I just wanted to die so I couldn't feel any pain, I opened the pills and I made sure I took them all with the beer I had bought. I thought about my mother most of the time and that was even more strange. I thought about my little brother, I imagined him saying Momma gone get you. I felt myself getting really sleepy, I was losing control of my body.

The next thing I knew, I was waking up with tubes everywhere. Where the hell am I? Am I dead? Am I in heaven? Who is this lady? Where is my momma?

Afterword

Writing this book had opened so many doors that have been closed for many years. I thought I was strong enough to share those memories without help. I was wrong because I have encountered many break downs and needed plenty of theraphy to close out this series due to P.T.S.D. However, I made it through and I have unlocked another level of peace in my mind. I pray that my story will help you turn your negatives into a positive and be the best you possible.

Biography

Danette McKinley has been a fighter all of her life. Born July 30th 1974 in Chicago, IL, she has faced and overcome many adversities, including coming from a broken family and entering the judicial system at a very young age.

Danette currently has seven children, including one that's deceased. She had her first child at the age of fourteen after suffering multiple forms of abuse. Danette has dedicated her life to changing the lives and views of the youth of today. She has performed multiple services and given countless donations to the Austin Township Community and has worked for other communities and organizations to help establish a healthier living environment for today's urban youth.

Through her love and passion for children and impoverished teens, in 2007, she founded Young Creative Minds (YCM) youth organization. Which has etched quite a reputation for itself?

She created and facilitated the famous Westside spelling bee within the Austin community. This event catered to the Chicago public school district to promote literacy, awareness and good sportsmanship among peers, as well as scholastic acceleration.

YCM landscaping service takes teenagers that were either on probation or paroled and gives them option to complete their community service through this program. They also have an opportunity to become employed for their services.

The community salute concert series is yet another innovative way to give back to her community. She orchestrated a free concert for under privileged children whom couldn't afford tickets to see their favorite artists.

Just to name a few of her many attributes Danette uses her past pains as her strength in order to pave a road for children and young adults that has or are currently traveling a path that she once traveled.

From speaking of past pains from abusive and non-cohesive relationships to dealing one on one with Chicago underground drug cartels, she continues to inspire young women and young men to be more than what the system has labeled them, which is another statistic.

Danette has received multiple accolades from city aldermen and even former Mayor Richard H. Daley. As long as she continues to be a pillar of the urban community and a champion for youth, she is sure to receive much more in the future.

1 Peter 4:8

And above all things be earnest in your love among yourselves, for love covers a multitude of sin.

Notes

www.ingramcontent.com/pod-product-compliance
Lightning Source LLC
Chambersburg PA
CBHW021412290426
44108CB00010B/502